Plague

A History of Pestilence and Pandemics

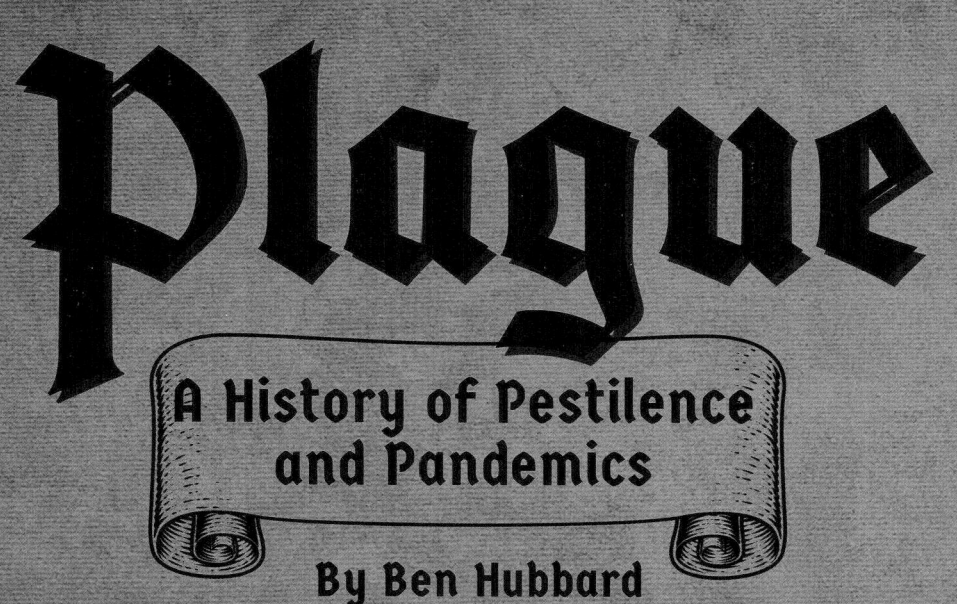

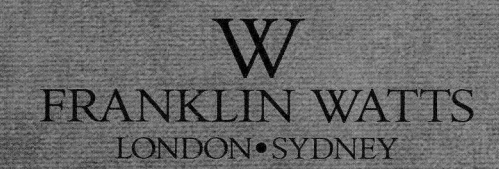

By Ben Hubbard

2 : A HISTORY OF DISEASE
4 : MALARIA
6 : PLAGUE OF ATHENS
8 : ANTONINE PLAGUE
10 : THE JUSTINIAN PLAGUE
12 : THE BLACK DEATH
14 : COCOLIZTLI EPIDEMIC
16 : GREAT PLAGUE OF LONDON
18 : TUBERCULOSIS
20 : CHOLERA PANDEMICS
22 : 1918 SPANISH FLU
24 : SMALLPOX
26 : HIV/AIDS
28 : TIMELINE OF DISEASES
30 : GLOSSARY
32 : INDEX

W

FRANKLIN WATTS
LONDON·SYDNEY

A HISTORY OF DISEASE

In late 2019, a mysterious new disease appeared in China. The main symptoms were fever, coughing and tiredness. It was spreading fast. Tiny airborne droplets from people sneezing, coughing or talking landed on surfaces and infected others.

In January 2020 new cases were reported in Thailand, Finland and the Philippines. In February the World Health Organization gave the disease a name: COVID-19. It is caused by the SARS-CoV-2 virus, which is related to coronaviruses found in bats and pangolins. Infected meat from these animals probably caused the outbreak. By the end of August 2020, COVID-19 had swept across the world, claiming over 750,000 lives. It was the new pandemic of our modern age.

What is a pandemic?
A pandemic is when an epidemic, an outbreak of an infectious disease, is spreading fast around the world. Pandemics have claimed many millions of lives throughout human history. Some pass, such as

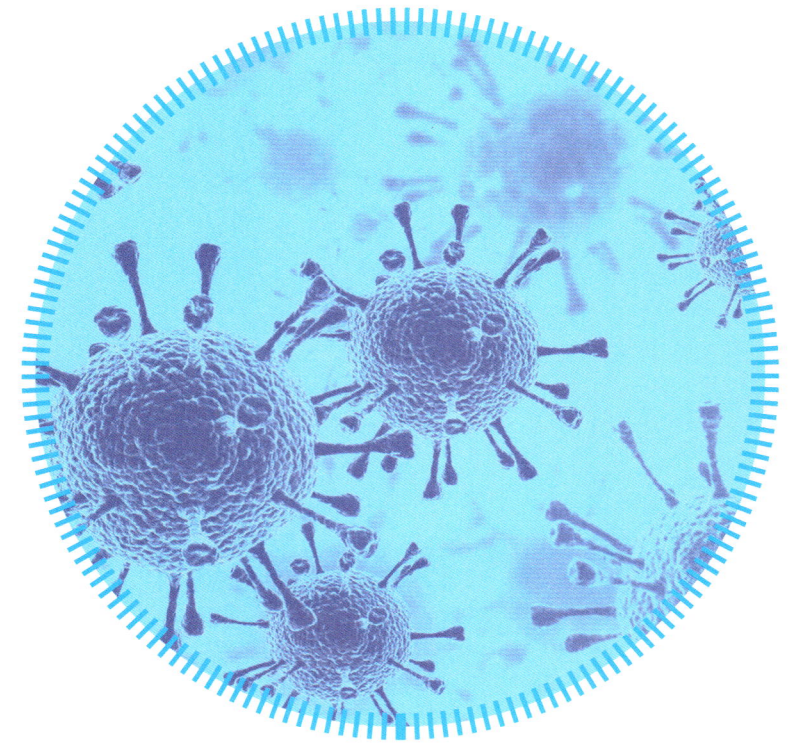

The spikes on a COVID-19 virus give its nickname of 'corona' or 'crown'.

Spanish Flu in 1918–19 (see pages 22–23). Other pandemics break out and stay, like cholera or HIV/AIDS (see pages 20–21/26–27).

Cholera thrives in overcrowded areas where sanitation is poor and people live in poverty. Most countries rid themselves of cholera in the early 20th century by building pipes and sewers to transport clean or dirty water to and from homes and other buildings. However, the disease persists in low-income countries where many people have no choice but to drink dirty water.

Fighting pandemics

Today, good sanitation seems an obvious way to prevent disease, along with self-isolation and 'social-distancing'. But science and medicine remain our greatest weapons in the fight against pandemics.

In the past, bloodletting, burning herbs and shaving a chicken's bottom and strapping it to your feet were all accepted as good ways to stop the spread of disease. Today advances in science help us understand disease much better, yet unscientific cures and ideas still pop up. Dangerous substances such as bleach were suggested as a cure for COVID-19 in 2020. Others chose to break self-isolation rules and not wear masks. Several governments worldwide caused thousands of unnecessary deaths by not preparing properly for the pandemic.

Meanwhile, those in hospitals and care homes worked all hours caring for people with COVID-19. It is these human actions, both good and bad, that are remembered when the world faces a disease that seems capable of destroying us all.

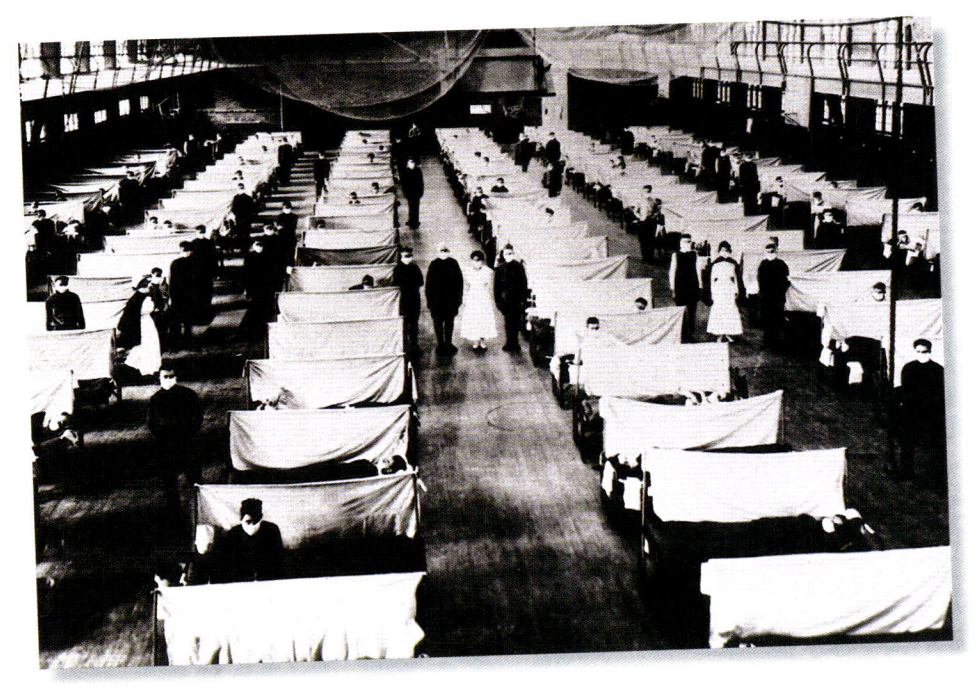

Hospitals could not accommodate the high numbers of patients during the 1918–19 Spanish Flu pandemic. Public spaces, such as this American school gym, were converted into wards screened off by bed sheets.

In many places in 2020, masks and social distancing became law in public places.

MALARIA
(30 MILLION YEARS AGO)

Malaria is one of the world's oldest and most deadly diseases. In the 20th century alone, malaria claimed as many as 300 million lives. Malaria is caused by the tiny parasite *Plasmodium* which is spread by the female of the bloodsucking insect, the Anopheles mosquito. When the mosquito bites a person infected with malaria it picks up the parasite and passes it on to the next person it bites. This is a terribly effective way for the disease to spread.

An ancient mosquito is pictured trapped inside amber, which is fossilised tree resin that was formed millions of years ago.

AMBER AND EGYPT

Mosquitoes carrying malaria have been found trapped in tree resin that is 20 million years old. Humans have probably always suffered from the disease but the first written record dates back to China in 2700 BCE, the ancient Egyptians in 1570 BCE and Mesopotamia in 200 BCE. Archaeologists have discovered that the Egyptian King Tutankhamun died from malaria and a broken leg around 3,000 years ago. Evidence of the disease was found in his mummified remains. It is also thought that the Egyptian Queen Cleopatra designed mosquito nets for her bed so that she could sleep safely at night.

Tutankhamun was buried in this tomb in 1323 BCE. His mummified remains were discovered and examined in 1922.

DESCRIPTION OF DISEASE

When a malaria-carrying mosquito bites someone, it injects the offspring of a *Plasmodium* parasite into the victim's bloodstream. These multiply in the person's liver before re-entering the bloodstream and killing red blood cells. The victim does not show symptoms for seven to 30 days but then falls ill with chills, fever, headaches, vomiting and diarrhoea. Death can follow if the person is not treated.

GREECE AND ROME

Malaria was a big problem in ancient Greece and Rome. Ancient Rome was badly hit after malarial mosquitoes reached Europe from Africa via Egypt. Romans performed ceremonies over the bodies of children who had died of malaria to stop them from returning from the dead. So many people died that some historians believe that a malaria epidemic in the 5th century contributed to the end of the Roman Empire.

CINCHONA TREE

Europeans introduced malaria to the Americas in the 16th century when they transported African slaves, infected with the disease, to work on the land. It was in Peru in the 17th century that Spanish missionaries noticed indigenous people used the bark of the cinchona tree to treat fevers. The missionaries then successfully tried this remedy on malaria sufferers. Cinchona later became the main ingredient of quinine, which is still used to treat malaria today.

The bark of the cinchona tree, shown here, was the only effective remedy for malaria for 300 years after its introduction into Western medicine.

MALARIA TODAY

Sadly, malaria continues to kill hundreds of thousands of people every year in low-income countries in Africa, Asia and South America where mosquitoes thrive. Since 2000, deaths have been going down due to better drugs to treat infected people and the use of bed nets sprayed with insecticides.

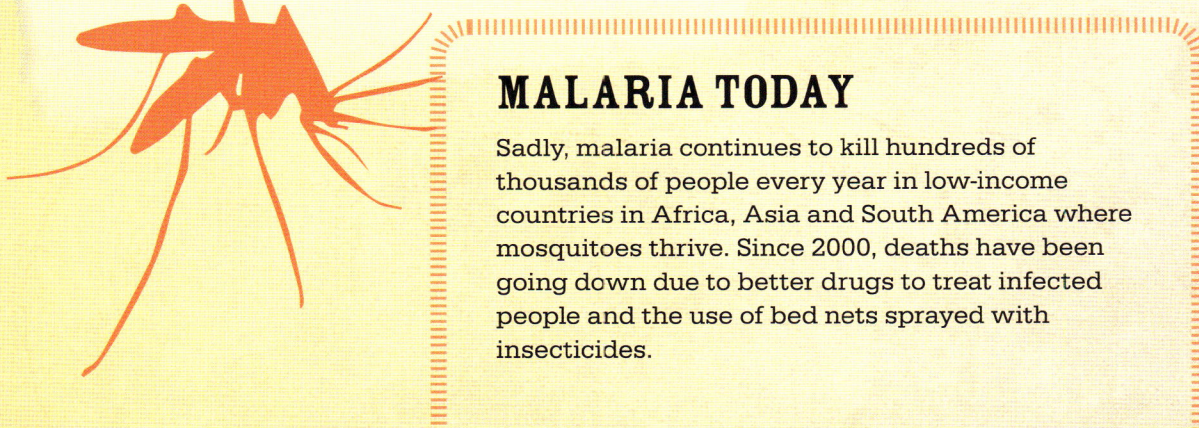

PLAGUE OF ATHENS

(GREECE, 430 BCE)

Disease often strikes civilisations at the worst possible moment. So it was with the Plague of Athens in 430 BCE. At that time, the city-state was already in crisis. Athens was being besieged by its great enemy Sparta during the Peloponnesian War (431–404 BCE). Trapped inside their tightly-confined city walls, Athenians were already terrified for their lives. But then, people from the city's port of Piraeus began suffering from a strange new sickness.

SYMPTOMS

The Greek historian Thucydides, who fell ill with the disease but later recovered, wanted future generations to be warned of its symptoms in case it struck again.

"Violent heats in the head; redness and inflammation of the eyes; throat and tongue quickly suffused with blood; breath became unnatural and fetid; sneezing and hoarseness; violent cough; vomiting; retching; violent convulsions; the body externally not so hot to the touch, nor yet pale; a livid colour inkling to red; breaking out in pustules and ulcers."

Thucydides, *History of the Peloponnesian War*

Alongside these symptoms, people also suffered from a terrible thirst that no amount of water could quench, diarrhoea, blindness and gangrene in their fingers, toes and genitals which sometimes caused them to drop off. Most victims died within a week and even vultures and dogs would not go near their corpses.

'Myrtis' is a reconstructed 11-year-old Athenian plague victim. Her skull was found among 150 men, women and children who were all hastily buried around 430 BCE.

Lysander (far right) was one of the Spartan generals who laid siege to Athens. He took control of the city in 404 BCE.

EARTHLY PLEASURES

A city with cramped housing and inadequate sanitation, Athens was ripe for an outbreak of disease. As the plague tore through the city, as many as 100,000 people died. Athens was famous for its great thinkers but as fear and death spread, residents lost their self-control. Believing they would all die, many turned to earthly pleasures, such as drinking alcohol. Others could not be bothered to give their dead family members respectful burials.

A 17th century painting of the Plague of Athens.

DISEASE UNKNOWN

The Plague of Athens probably arrived with people aboard trading ships from Ethiopia and Libya, which docked at Piraeus. Even today, modern scientists cannot be certain which disease caused the Plague of Athens. Some suggestions include typhus, typhoid, smallpox, measles, anthrax, influenza, cholera or the plague – or a combination of these diseases. We may never know. We do know that whatever the disease was, it devastated Athens. The city-state later lost the Peloponnesian War to Sparta.

The port of Piraeus is pictured with the Athenian 'Long Walls' leading up to the city.

Roman legionaries march on one of the many roads which connected the Empire.

ANTONINE PLAGUE

(ROMAN EMPIRE, CE 165-180)

In CE 165, the mighty Roman Empire was at the height of its power. Rome controlled a vast amount of land that stretched from England in the west, to Syria in the east. And then, disaster struck. Roman legionaries returning from campaigns in the east brought with them a terrible, infectious disease. As they marched back towards the capital on the Roman roads designed to join up the Empire, they infected its people with disease.

DISEASE SEIZES ROME

In Rome, co-emperors Lucius Verus (reigned 161–169) and Marcus Aurelius Antoninus (reigned 161–180) summoned the famous Greek doctor Galen (129–c.210). But Galen could not explain the disease that was ravaging Rome. At its peak, as many as 2,000 people died a day in Rome, probably including Emperor Lucius Verus himself. Soon there were not enough magistrates to run local councils, nor farmers to produce food. So many soldiers died that the borders of the Roman Empire became vulnerable to attack.

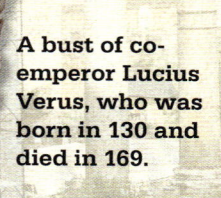

A bust of co-emperor Lucius Verus, who was born in 130 and died in 169.

FEAR AND REDEMPTION

As the disease swept across the Roman Empire, fear and panic took hold. Many prayed to Apollo, the Roman god of health and healing. Others wore amulets to protect themselves. But just as Rome reached its most desperate moment, the pandemic began to fade. Emperor Marcus Aurelius Antoninus, who gave the outbreak its name, then took practical steps to save the Empire. He recruited slaves and gladiators as legionaries, gave abandoned farms to migrants from outside the Empire, and filled council vacancies with the sons of freed slaves. Gradually, Rome recovered.

Emperor Marcus Aurelius Antoninus lived between 121 and 180.

SYMPTOMS OF THE PLAGUE

Although Galen could not cure the disease afflicting the Empire, he did describe its gruesome symptoms. It began with fever, chills, vomiting, coughing, black diarrhoea and very smelly breath. Soon, black pimples appeared on the inside and outside of a victim's body. Sometimes these spots were dry and at other times filled with pus. Pimples that burst scabbed over and then fell off, were coughed up or excreted from the body. In two to three weeks, victims would either die or recover.

Galen was one of the most influential physicians of the ancient world.

MAYBE SMALLPOX

Many modern scientists believe the Antonine Plague was an outbreak of smallpox (see pages 24–25). Some say it was a measles pandemic. It may have spread to the Roman Empire from China along the Silk Road trade route. Some believe Roman legionaries caught the disease during the siege of Seleucia, in Iraq. At the time a story went round that a Roman soldier in Babylon (modern Iraq) allowed the disease to escape when he opened a coffin in the Temple of Apollo.

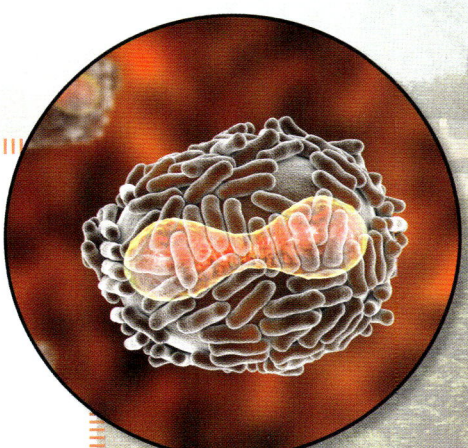

A microscopic image of the smallpox virus is shown here, and its effect on the skin, opposite.

9

THE JUSTINIAN PLAGUE
(CONSTANTINOPLE, 541-544)

In 541, people in Constantinople (modern Istanbul) began having terrible nightmares. They imagined headless figures cloaked in black rowing across the sea towards them. Then, they fell ill with fever and painful, pus-filled swellings in the armpits, neck and groin. This was followed by hallucinations, diarrhoea, vomiting blood and death. Before long, thousands of people in Constantinople were dying of this new, nameless disease. Today we know it simply as the plague.

Here, monks pray for a gravedigger suffering from the Justinian Plague.

FIRST PLAGUE PANDEMIC

The people of Constantinople did not know it, but their city was being ravaged by the first known plague pandemic in history. The plague was caused by the microscopic bacterium *Yersinia pestis*, which entered the human body via the bite of an infected flea. Flea-infested rats aboard ships carried the disease to European and Middle-Eastern port cities from Asia or Africa. No-one is sure where the plague started, but its first pandemic lasted two years and killed at least 25 million people.

A microscopic image of the *Yersinia pestis* bacteria.

PLAGUE FORMS

The plague is caused by *Yersinia pestis* bacteria, but the form it takes in humans depends on the way they become infected. There are three main forms:

Bubonic plague is spread by flea bites. Its symptoms include vomiting, fever, black swellings, called buboes, and gangrene.

Pneumonic plague can be easily spread from person to person through sneezing or coughing. Its symptoms include fever, breathlessness and death from fluid in the lungs (pneumonia).

Septicemic plague is spread by the bites of infected fleas and causes the bloodstream to be overrun by *Yersinia pestis* bacteria. Its symptoms include tiredness, fever, internal bleeding and a rapid death.

CONSTANTINOPLE CORPSES

The plague ravaged Constantinople with such ferocity that authorities had trouble disposing of the dead. Bodies were thrown into mass graves, piled up in towers and loaded onto boats. The stench of rotting flesh was everywhere, as rich and poor alike succumbed to the disease. Those not suffering from the plague were kept busy burying or caring for those who were.

Justinian I was emperor of the Eastern Roman Empire (shown in the map above). He lived between 483 and 565.

JUSTINIAN I (REIGNED 527-565)

The capital of the Eastern Roman Empire, Constantinople, was a trading centre and so its port provided perfect conditions for an outbreak of the plague. Emperor Justinian I caught the disease and although he recovered, the plague dealt his empire a crippling blow. A Constantinople scholar called Procopius declared that the plague was a punishment from God for Justinian's cruel behaviour and for over-taxing his people.

THE BLACK DEATH

(EUROPE, ASIA, NORTH AFRICA, 1347-1352)

In 1348 bad omens were reported in France. A comet was said to hover over Paris and, three days later, the Black Death struck the city. Arriving from the port of Marseilles, probably from Asia, this plague obliterated the capital's population. The city leaders could not cope with the death toll, which reached more than 700 a day. The city's morgue and cemeteries overflowed; soon bodies were simply left to rot in the street.

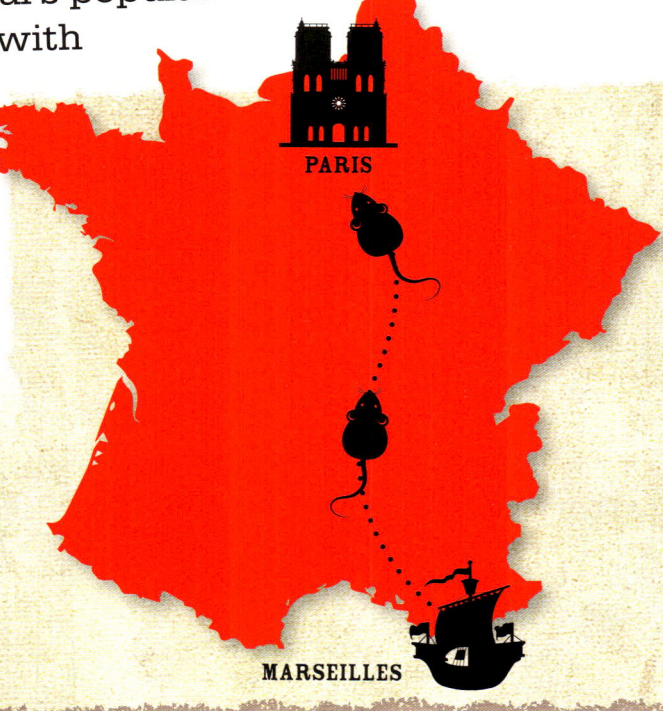

PARIS

MARSEILLES

The people of Tournai, in Belgium, bury victims of the Black Death.

CRITICAL CONTAGION

As with the Justinian Plague in 541, symptoms of the Black Death included black buboes in a victim's armpits, neck and groin, fever and vomiting blood. It was bubonic plague, spread by flea-infected rats. When the rats died of the disease, the fleas jumped off their bodies and bit humans instead. Between 1347 and 1351, the Black Death spread across Europe and killed over 50 million people. The upside was that although it left nations mourning their dead, those that survived were more able to fight for better living conditions. With fewer people, there was more housing and food to go round and wages went up, as working people were in short supply.

PLAGUE DOCTORS

There was no cure for the Black Death, but many 'Plague Doctors' were willing to try. The doctors fed plague victims foul-tasting concoctions and lanced their boils. Most quickly fell victim to the same disease they were trying to cure, as did many Augustinian Nuns who did their best to comfort the dying.

An illustration of a 14th century Plague Doctor with one of his concoctions.

THE DANSE MACABRE

The *Danse Macabre*, or Dance of Death (above), became a popular theme for paintings and prints after people witnessed so much death during the pandemic. It warned people that no matter how wealthy or poor they were, death comes to all. Fear of dying from the Black Death led many to flee Paris or to lock themselves away to avoid catching the disease.

In later centuries, Plague Doctors dressed in protective clothing that included bird masks like this one. The beaks of bird masks contained sweet-smelling flowers to combat the stench of death, as well as items such as garlic that were believed to protect the wearer from disease.

Here, the Spanish conquistador Hernán Cortés captures the Aztec capital, Tenochtitlan, in 1521.

COCOLIZTLI EPIDEMIC

(MEXICO, 1545-1548)

In 1519 Spanish conquistadors began a violent conquest of the Aztec Empire in modern-day Mexico. Thousands of Aztecs were killed during the invasion. But the numbers were small compared to those who died from diseases introduced by the Spanish. One mysterious disease, called cocoliztli (after the Aztec word for pestilence), killed as many as 13 million Aztecs – or 80 per cent of the population – during a 1545 epidemic. It remains one of the worst outbreaks in history.

COCOLIZTLI SYMPTOMS

Neither Aztec nor Spanish doctors knew what cocoliztli was when it struck the local population. The disease lasted three to five days and started with a high fever, headaches, red eyes and an unquenchable thirst. Then the skin and eyes turned yellow, pus-filled boils appeared around the neck and face and black urine and bloody diarrhoea began. Ulcers on the lips and genitals and intense chest and stomach pain followed. The few that survived were left thin and weak and often the illness returned.

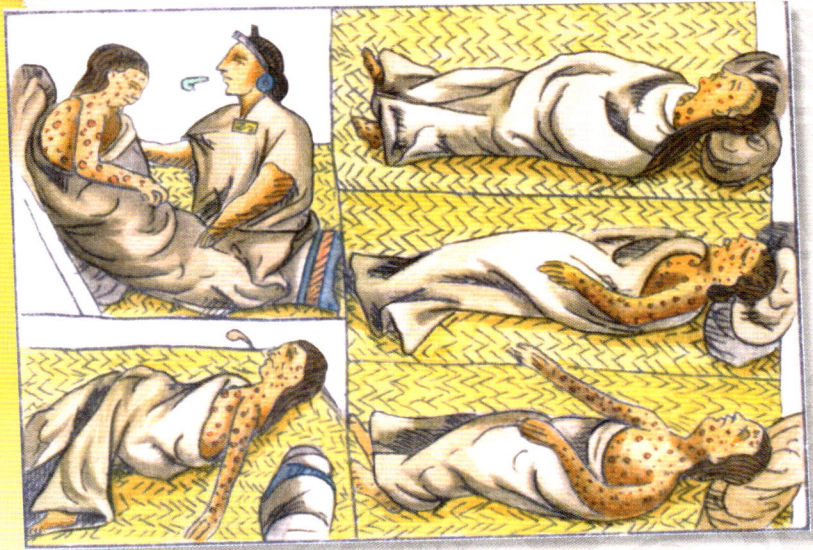

Sufferers of the cocoliztli epidemic are pictured in this 16th century Florentine Codex.

DITCHES OF DEATH

The 1545 cocoliztli epidemic lasted for five years. Only four million of the 17 million Aztec population survived. Then, in 1576, cocoliztli struck again. The disease quickly spread, killing half the remaining population. A Franciscan friar called Fray Juan de Torquemada (c.1563–1624) wrote: "In the cities and large towns, big ditches were dug, and from morning to sunset the priests did nothing else but carry the dead bodies and throw them into the ditches."

Juan de Torquemada wrote a history of the Aztec people following the Spanish invasion.

CONFUSING COCOLIZTLI

Cocoliztli confused doctors at the time and for hundreds of years afterwards. The Spanish accidentally introduced diseases such as smallpox, measles, mumps and typhus to Mexico, but none of these matched the symptoms of cocoliztli. Then, in 2018, a study of DNA from buried Aztec bodies revealed bacteria called *Salmonella enterica*, which can cause symptoms that match those of cocoliztli. Salmonella has never caused an outbreak as deadly as cocoliztli before or since but remains the most likely cause of the epidemic at the moment.

AZTEC-KILLING DISEASES

Three huge epidemics swept through the Aztec population, brought to Central America by the Spanish invaders and settlers. This table shows their dates and how many died.

1520–1527	Smallpox epidemic	5–8 million killed
1545–1550	Cocoliztli epidemic	5–15 million killed
1576–1580	Cocoliztli epidemic	2 million killed

GREAT PLAGUE OF LONDON

(LONDON, 1665-1666)

The plague which ravaged Europe, Asia and North Africa in the 14th century (see pages 12–13) never completely disappeared. Outbreaks continued for several centuries. One such outbreak in England began in the London suburb of Saint Giles-in-the-Fields in 1665. Before long, the outbreak had turned into a major epidemic. Suddenly it was killing thousands across London's poverty-stricken suburbs. King Charles II (1630–1685) and other nobles immediately fled the capital, leaving ordinary Londoners to face this 'Great Plague' alone.

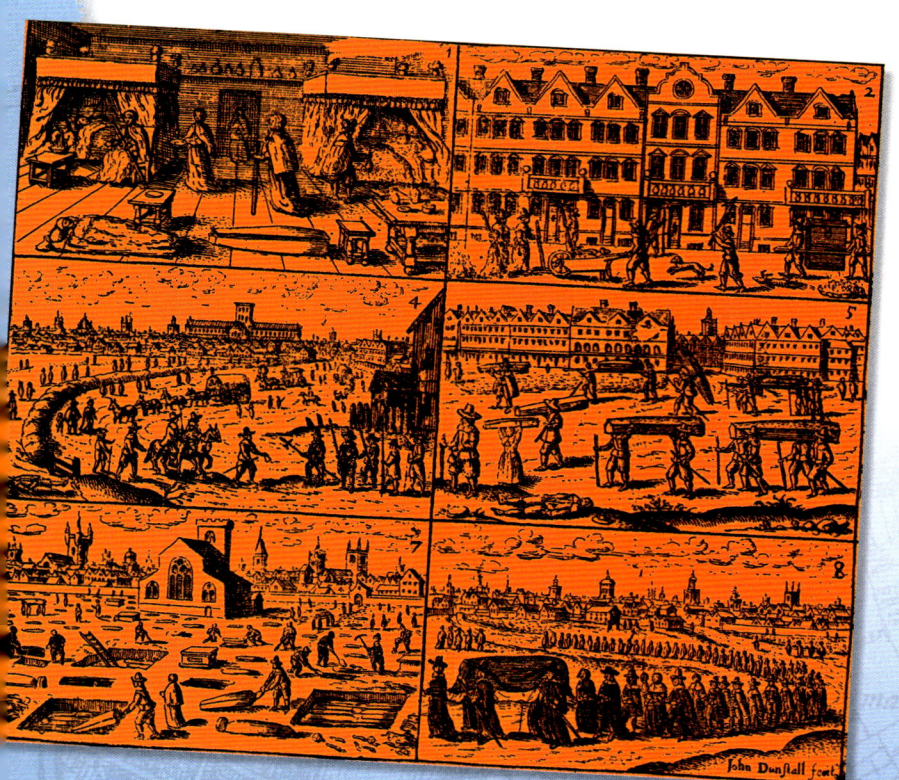

DESCRIPTION OF DISEASE

English novelist Daniel Defoe (1660–1731) used childhood memories and research to write about the Great Plague in *A Journal of the Plague Year*, published in 1722:
"… some were immediately overwhelmed with it [the plague], and it came to violent fevers, vomitings, insufferable headaches, pains in the back, and so up to ravings and ragings with those pains. Others with swellings and tumours in the neck or groin, or armpits, which till they could be broke put them into insufferable agonies and torment; while others, as I have observed, were silently infected …"

Daniel Defoe wrote about the Great Plague of London in 1722.

BURNING BAD AIR

In the 17th century, no-one understood the plague. No connection was made between the spread of disease and overcrowded, unhealthy living conditions. London at that time was awash with its own filth: rubbish and human waste was simply thrown into the streets, attracting rats. No-one realised that the rats carrying infected fleas spread the plague as people believed that bad air vapours, called miasmas, were the cause. Hoping to drive away the bad air, people were ordered to light fires in the streets.

Fires were kept burning in London night and day to try to stop the plague.

CORPSES AND QUARANTINE

While the cause of the plague was unknown, quarantine was used to try to stop its spread. In London, plague houses had a big red cross painted on the front door as well as the words: 'Lord Have Mercy Upon Us'. The family of the sick were locked inside for 40 days, their door guarded by a watchman. At night, men called out "Bring out your dead" as they travelled the streets of London with their carts. The churchyards and cemeteries of London filled up fast.

Watchmen such as this one accepted bribes so that plague sufferers could visit the pub.

DESERTING DEATH

With thousands succumbing to bubonic plague every week, the streets of London became almost deserted in 1665. Official figures from the time claim 70,000 died, but it was probably closer to 100,000. In the autumn the death toll slowed, although plague cases kept occurring until mid-1666. No one knows why this particular plague epidemic died out.

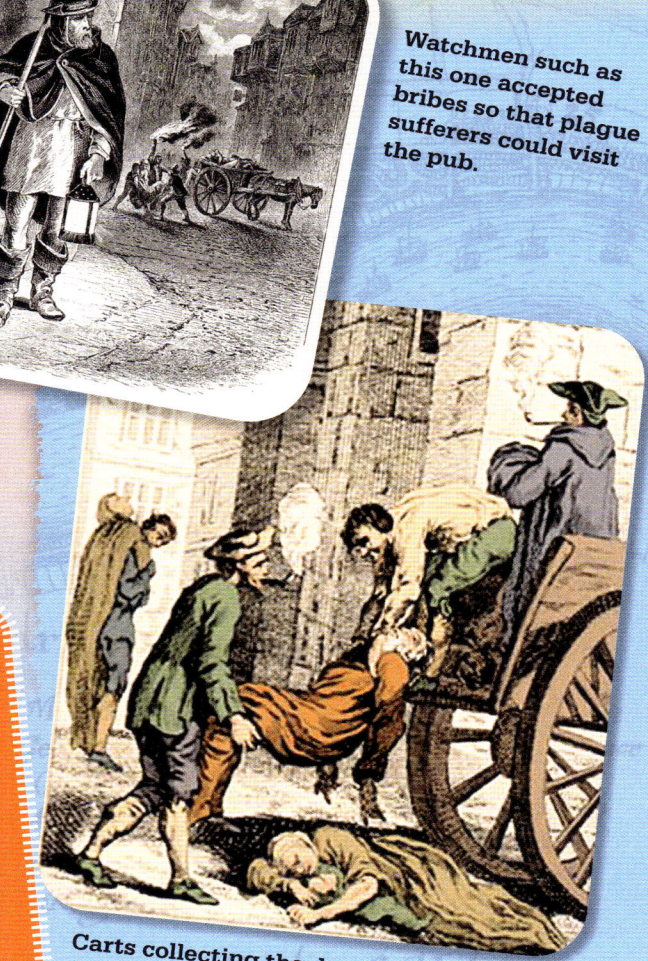

Carts collecting the dead were a common feature of London's Great Plague.

17

TUBERCULOSIS

(WORLD, STONE AGE - PRESENT DAY)

Tuberculosis (TB) is an ancient disease that has been infecting humans since the Stone Age. Doctors from ancient Egypt, Greece, Rome and China all wrote about TB: it became known as 'wasting', the 'white plague' and 'consumption'. This is because the disease 'consumes' its victims, causing them to become pale and thin and start coughing up bright-red blood. Millions worldwide are still affected by TB today.

ROMANTIC DISEASE

Tuberculosis did not suddenly appear and kill millions, like the plague or cholera. However, it has killed more people than both of these diseases. Between 1600 and 1800, tuberculosis caused 25 per cent of all deaths in Europe. It peaked during the 19th century, a time when it was believed that TB affected sensitive people with delicate natures after several artistic people, including the poet John Keats, died of the disease. It became fashionable for wealthy young women to be thin and pale, as if they were suffering from TB.

Marie Duplessis was a Parisian socialite who died of TB at age 23.

VAMPIRES AND BLOODLETTING

While TB may have had a romantic appeal among some wealthy Europeans, it caused horrible suffering for the poor. During the 19th century, as more and more people moved from the countryside to towns and cities to find work, homes became overcrowded and turned into slums. This meant people caught TB easily as they were already unhealthy and lived too closely together. There was no cure at that time, and treatments included bloodletting, horse-riding and opiates. In parts of the USA, people performed rituals over graves so that those who had died from TB would not come back as vampires and bite family members.

INFECTIOUS SCIENCE

By the end of the 19th century, there were some scientific breakthroughs in TB research. In 1882, German doctor Robert Koch (1843–1910) discovered that the disease was caused by the bacterium *Mycobacterium tuberculosis*. This proved that TB was an infectious disease, passed through the air by breathing in infected droplets when someone with TB coughed, sneezed or talked.

The bacterium *Mycobacterium tuberculosis* is shown here through a microscope.

German physician Robert Koch discovered the causes of the infectious diseases TB, cholera and anthrax.

SANATORIUMS

In the late 19th century, hospitals called sanatoriums were built to quarantine TB sufferers. Built in the countryside, sanatoriums offered patients clean air and healthy food to help their bodies fight TB, while also isolating them from the general public. Sanatoriums closed in the mid-20th century, when antibiotic drugs were developed to treat the disease. However, despite these drugs and the BCG vaccine, TB still infects millions every year. Scientists hope to eradicate the disease by 2030.

Sanatoriums were countryside retreats where TB sufferers could recuperate.

CHOLERA PANDEMICS

(WORLD, 1817–1923)

Cholera was a small-time killer before the 19th century. But in 1817, there was a deadly outbreak in India that spread around the world along trade routes. For over a hundred years, cholera caused seven deadly pandemics and killed tens of millions. It was a shocking disease for which the cause and cure were unknown. Victims of the disease were struck down with terrible vomiting and diarrhoea. They turned grey and ghost-like before they died.

BORDERS AND BODIES

In 1830, alarmed European nations took drastic action. Governments tried to prevent the disease reaching them by restricting visitors. In Moscow, Russia, troops stopped people from entering the city. In Britain, riots broke out due to rumours that doctors were giving patients cholera so that they could conduct research on their corpses. In France, many believed the rich were using cholera to kill off the poor.

In 1831, people in Russia's St Petersburg protested at having to be quarantined against cholera. Tsar Nicholas I himself helped quell the crowds.

Here, the Grim Reaper is seen above a crowd of people infected with cholera.

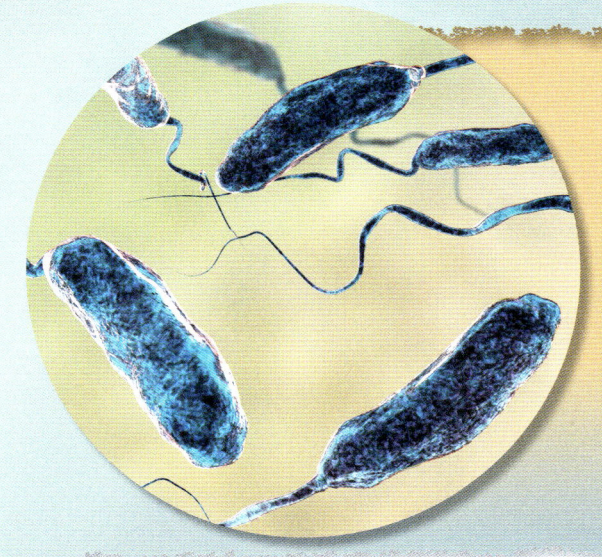

THE POOR AND IMMIGRANTS

Fear, panic and hatred accompanied the cholera pandemics in western Europe. Because the worst outbreaks occurred in overcrowded slums with large immigrant populations, foreigners were often blamed for the disease. In reality, the outbreaks were caused by a lack of clean drinking water and good drains. Eventually scientists discovered that cholera is caused by the bacterium *Vibrio cholerae,* carried in dirty water.

SNOW'S PUMP

Some understood the link between cholera and bad living conditions. In the 1840s, British doctor John Snow (1813–1858) wondered if water infected with cholera was getting into drinking water. He collected evidence that a lot of cholera deaths were linked to people drawing water from the Broad Street water pump in London's Soho. It took a lot of effort to convince others of his findings but in 1854 officials agreed to put the pump out of action by removing its handle, and cases of cholera dropped. Later it was discovered that sewage was leaking into the water well.

Ordinary Londoners were forced to share dirty water from the same source.

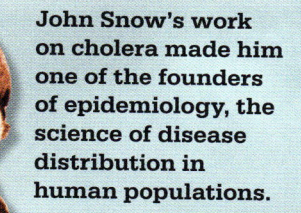

John Snow's work on cholera made him one of the founders of epidemiology, the science of disease distribution in human populations.

CHOLERA TODAY

Snow's discovery that cholera spread in dirty water helped countries to eradicate the disease by building sewers for waste water and cleaning up drinking water. However, cholera still persists today in low-income countries. Between one and four million people catch cholera every year but most of them survive, if they receive medical treatment. Still, between 21,000 and 143,000 of them die due to poor living conditions and lack of healthcare. For this reason, cholera is called 'the forgotten pandemic'.

1918 SPANISH FLU (WORLD, 1918-1920)

Influenza, or 'the flu', is a contagious virus spread through the air by sneezes and coughs. Usually the flu is a winter illness from which most people recover. But in 1918, an outbreak of influenza became one of the deadliest global pandemics in history. In just over a year, 'Spanish Flu' infected over 500 million people worldwide and claimed between 50 and 100 million lives. It became known as Spanish Flu because Spain was the first country to report on the disease.

These police officers in Seattle, USA, in 1918, are wearing protective masks made by the Red Cross.

OUTBREAK AND SYMPTOMS

Occurring in three waves, Spanish Flu first broke out in Camp Funston in Kansas, USA in March 1918. The camp trained soldiers who were about to be sent to fight in the First World War (1914–18) in France and Belgium. The first wave of the flu was mild and victims recovered quickly, but the second wave was worse. In just hours, victims developed symptoms that included the skin turning blue, bleeding from the eyes, ears and nose and suffocation from fluid in the lungs (pneumonia). Death usually occurred within two days.

Spanish Flu sufferers are pictured here at a US army hospital in Aix-les-Bains, France.

ACROSS SEAS AND CONTINENTS

The second wave of Spanish Flu spread quickly as infected people travelled in crowded ships and trains across seas and continents. Soon, around one-third of the world's population was infected. In Africa, people dug trenches for the corpses overflowing from cemeteries; villages in India became deserted as the virus killed over 12 million people. Then, just as the world could take no more, a third wave occurred in late 1919. However, by the next spring, Spanish Flu had died out.

Red Cross workers in St Louis, Missouri, USA, carry a patient into an ambulance during the Spanish Flu Epidemic.

MOST AT RISK

Soldiers returning from the First World War probably brought Spanish Flu to Australia and New Zealand. It soon spread to indigenous people, resulting in a death rate four times higher than the rest of the population. This is probably because they had poor access to healthcare and bad living conditions. In Australia and New Zealand, as elsewhere, Spanish Flu killed far more young people than older people. Scientists think this may be because the immune system of young people over-reacted to the virus, leading to deadly health complications.

The New Zealand cargo ship Talune brought the Spanish Flu to Samoa after it was not quarantined in dock and sick passengers were allowed to disembark.

INFLUENZA STRAINS

In 2005, scientists worked out that Spanish Flu was an influenza A: a lethal virus which passes to humans from animals. More specifically, Spanish Flu was an avian (bird) H1N1 virus that caused the lungs to fill with fluid and bring about pneumonia. In 2009 people around the world became very concerned about another H1N1 flu with the nickname 'swine flu'. Fortunately this flu did not become a pandemic.

SMALLPOX (WORLD, 1980)

In 1980, the World Health Organization made an amazing announcement: smallpox had been completely eradicated from the face of the Earth. In the long history of people's struggle against disease, this was a headline worth celebrating. Smallpox was one of the world's worst diseases. It had caused suffering for thousands of years, bringing disfigurement and death to hundreds of millions. But now, smallpox had been beaten by science.

Smallpox victims are shown being treated in this picture.

SEVERE SYMPTOMS

Caused by the variola virus, the symptoms of smallpox were severe. It could take up to 19 days for them to arrive, starting with a high fever, crippling pain, headaches and vomiting. Then, red sores called pox erupted on the face and body. The sores filled with pus and formed a scab. After about three weeks the scabs fell off, often leaving pockmarks and scars.

HISTORICAL SPREAD

Smallpox outbreaks first originated in the ancient world. Epidemics ravaged Japan in the 6th century and struck Africa, Spain and Portugal during the 7th century. Movements of people, such as the 11th century crusades and the Spanish attacks on the Aztec Empire from 1519 (see pages 14–15) spread smallpox around the world. In the 16th century, smallpox was Europe's most feared disease and epidemics struck repeatedly until the end of the 18th century. It also had a devastating effect on aboriginal Australians during the 19th century, when European settlers brought the disease to Australia.

Aboriginal Australians are shown being given the smallpox vaccination.

POCKMARKED BY POX

A famous sufferer of smallpox was Queen Elizabeth I. She caught the disease in 1562 and was wrapped in scarlet cloth to heal the red sores on her face. This had no effect, of course, and although she survived, her face was heavily scarred by pockmarks. As Elizabeth I believed her beauty was linked to her power to govern the country, her servants hid her scars with heavy, white, lead-based face paint. This almost certainly caused the lead poisoning which led to Elizabeth's hair and memory loss, tiredness, stomach problems and early death.

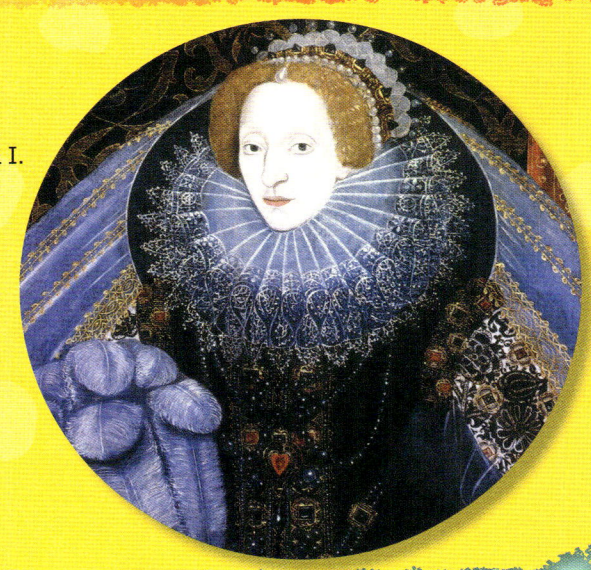

SMALLPOX VACCINE

Smallpox sufferers became contagious from the moment their first sores appeared. Then, droplets from a sneeze or cough were enough to infect someone else. Early experiments in Turkey proved that giving a mild dose of the disease to a healthy person could make them immune. In 1796, English doctor Edward Jenner (1749–1823) took this a step further when he developed a smallpox vaccine based on cowpox, a similar but milder disease. It worked. During the 19th century, Jenner's vaccine became compulsory in most countries.

Here, Edward Jenner examines a baby with smallpox.

HIV/AIDS

(WORLD, 1981-PRESENT)

In 1981, doctors in New York began noticing a strange increase in rare types of pneumonia and cancer, mainly in gay men. Soon drug addicts and haemophiliacs were also affected. These groups, and others, were all suffering from a disease of the immune system. In 1982 doctors called this condition 'acquired immunodeficiency syndrome' (AIDS), and the following year they discovered the virus that was causing it: the human immunodeficiency virus (HIV). Over 40 years later, about 76 million people worldwide have been infected by HIV and about 33 million people have died of HIV/AIDS. It is one of the worst pandemics in human history.

The HIV virus is shown here under a microscope.

THE FIRST CASES

Scientists think HIV came from West African chimpanzees around the turn of the 20th century. The chimpanzees were infected with a form of the virus which spread to the hunters who ate their meat. Over decades, the virus mutated into HIV in humans. In 1959, the disease was first detected in a man from the Democratic Republic of Congo.

GLOBAL SPREAD

HIV can be passed from one person to another in blood and other body fluids, but not saliva. Unprotected sex, blood transfusions, childbirth and sharing needles to inject drugs are the main ways HIV is spread. In the 1970s, HIV/AIDS appeared for the first time in the USA before the number of cases exploded in the 1980s. By 1990, over eight million people had been infected worldwide.

An AIDS poster tells people not to 'die of ignorance' in the 1980s.

SYMPTOMS

When someone first catches HIV, they may have a fever, a rash, swollen lymph nodes, mouth ulcers and an inflamed throat. In the next stage of the disease, the virus destroys CD4 (or T) cells which fight germs. This stage can last for years, gradually weakening the immune system to become AIDS. This means the person has a very weak immune system, unable to fight off disease or cancers. Symptoms linked to AIDS include weight loss, night sweats, fever, fatigue, sores, diarrhoea, pneumonia and skin blotches. Luckily today, if someone has a positive blood test for HIV, doctors can give them medicines to prevent them progressing to AIDS.

Marchers in Minnesota, USA, in 2013, call for people not to stigmatise those suffering from HIV/AIDS.

STIGMA AND DISCRIMINATION

Panic, fear and prejudice surrounded the 1980s outbreak of HIV/AIDS. Gay men were blamed for its spread and many people incorrectly believed they could be infected from toilet seats or a kiss. This meant that people were terrified to tell anyone if they had contracted the virus. In the 1990s, it became known that celebrities such as the singer, Freddie Mercury, and the basketball star, Magic Johnson (left), had HIV/AIDS. Slowly, with education and safe sex campaigns, understanding of the disease, including that not only gay sex can spread it, has changed people's views and brought down the number of infections. Freddie Mercury died of AIDS in 1991 but Magic Johnson survived by taking anti-HIV drugs to slow the disease.

27

TIMELINE OF DISEASES

Many millions of humans have died from the diseases that have afflicted civilisations since the dawn of history. The following timeline shows the numbers estimated to have died. But the exact numbers can never truly be known, especially for those diseases far back in time. Today, the numbers of those who die from diseases such as COVID-19 are easier to count, but sometimes deliberately made unclear. In 2020, some leaders tried to blur the numbers of the COVID-19 dead to try to make their leadership look better. The good news, however, is that the number who recovered from the disease far outweighed those who died from it.

Tuberculosis
Date: Stone age–present
Location: World
Fatalities: 1.5 million per year (2018 figure)

Plague of Athens
Date: 430 BCE
Location: Greece
Fatalities: 75,000–100,000

Antonine Plague
Date: CE 165–180
Location: Roman Empire
Fatalities: 5 million

Justinian Plague
Date: 541–542
Location: Constantinople
Fatalities: 25 million

The Black Death
Date: 1346–1353
Location: Europe, Asia, North Africa
Fatalities: 25–50 million

Smallpox
Date: 1520–1527
Location: Mexico
Fatalities: 5–8 million

Cocoliztli Epidemic
Date: 1545–1578
Location: Mexico
Fatalities: 7–17 million

Great Plague of London
Date: 1665–1666
Location: England
Fatalities: 68,596–100,000

Yellow Fever
Date: 1793
Location: Philadelphia, USA
Fatalities: 5,000

Third Cholera Pandemic
Date: 1852–1860
Location: World
Fatalities: 1 million

Third Plague Pandemic
Date: 1894–1922
Location: World
Fatalities: 12 million

Russian Flu
Date: 1889–1890
Location: Russia, World
Fatalities: 1 million

Smallpox
Date: 20th century
Location: World
Fatalities: 500 million

Malaria
Date: 20th century
Location: World
Fatalities: 150–300 million

1918 Spanish Flu
Date: 1918–1919
Location: World
Fatalities: 50–100 million

Asian Flu
Date: 1957–1958
Location: China, Singapore, Hong Kong, United States
Fatalities: 1.1 million

Hong Kong Flu
Date: 1968
Location: Asia, Australia, Europe, the Americas
Fatalities: 1–4 million

HIV/AIDS
Date: 1981-present
Location: World
Fatalities: 35+ million

SARS
Date: 2002–2003
Location: the Americas, Europe, Asia
Fatalities: 774

Swine Flu
Date: 2009–2010
Location: World
Fatalities: 284,000

Ebola
Date: 2014–2016
Location: Africa, World
Fatalities: 11,325

COVID-19
Date: 2019
Location: World
Fatalities: 750,00 and counting

GLOSSARY

Americas The area that falls inside the continents of North and South America.

Amulet A piece of jewellery thought to give protection against evil or disease.

Anopheles mosquito A tiny bloodsucking fly that can pass on malaria via its bite. Only the female sucks blood.

Augustinian nun A religious order of nuns named after 5th century Saint Augustine of Hippo.

Bacterium/bacteria A single-celled microorganism that takes a round, spiral or rod-shape and can cause disease in humans.

Bloodletting The process of bleeding a patient using leeches or by making a cut.

City-state A city and surrounding area that forms its own independent state.

Comet An object from space made up of ice and dust with a 'tail' of gas and dust.

Conquistador A 16th-century Spanish soldier who helped colonise Mexico and Peru for Spain.

Contagious A contagious disease spreads easily from one person to another.

Crusade Medieval military expeditions made by Christian Europeans to seize the Holy Land in the Middle East from Muslims.

Decimate Destroy, kill or drastically reduce something.

Earthly pleasures Pleasures sought by the human body rather than spiritual pleasures, or pleasures of the mind.

Eradicate Destroy completely.

Excrete To expel something as waste.

Gangrene The death of soft human tissue from the loss of blood, resulting in rot and decay.

Haemophilia An inherited bleeding disorder where blood does not clot properly. In the 1970s and 1980s many people with haemophilia became infected with HIV/AIDS due to treatments involving blood products.

Indigenous A native person of a country or place.

Insecticide A substance made of chemicals used to kill insects.

Legionary A soldier of the ancient Roman army.

Lymph node A small round swelling in the human lymphatic system, which rescues fluids and proteins that have escaped from the blood and returns them to the circulatory system.

Measles An infectious disease that causes a fever and red rash.

Missionary A person who goes to a foreign country to convert people to their religion.

Mutate To change into something else, such as a new form.

Nodule A small hard swollen lump on the human body, often containing pus.

Omen An event or sign that people believe shows something good or bad is about to happen.

Opiate A drug containing opium as its main ingredient.

Parasite An organism that survives by living on or inside a bigger organism.

Peloponnesian War (431-404 BCE) A war fought between the Greek city-states of Sparta and Athens.

Pestilence An epidemic disease that is highly contagious.

Pustule A pus-filled spot.

Quarantine A period where humans and animals are placed in a place of isolation to prevent them catching or spreading disease.

Quinine A medicine taken from the cinchona tree that is used to treat malaria.

Sanitation Providing clean drinking water and disposing of sewage to prevent disease.

Siege The surrounding of a city or fortress by an army with the aim of forcing those inside to surrender.

Slave A person kept in captivity and forced to work for free.

Slum A poor, crowded area of a city with unhealthy living conditions, especially bad housing.

Stigma A mark of shame or disgrace that is given to a person.

Stone Age The historical period between around 3.3 million years ago and 8,000 BCE.

Symptom A physical feature in the human body which shows disease is present.

Ulcer An open sore either inside the body or outside, on the skin.

Virus A microscopic infective organism that can replicate inside the cells of living hosts and cause disease.

INDEX

anthrax 7, 19
Aztecs 14–15, 25
bacteria,
   Mycobacterium tuberculosis 19
   Salmonella enterica 15
   Vibrio cholerae 21
   Yersinia pestis 10–11
cholera 2, 7, 18–21, 28
Cocoliztli Epidemic 14–15, 28
conquistadors 14–15
consumption 18–19
Egypt, ancient 4–5, 18
First World War 22–23
Greece, ancient 5–8, 18

HIV/AIDS 2, 26–27, 29
Jenner, Edward 25
Koch, Robert 19
malaria 4–5, 9, 29
measles 7, 9, 15
parasite, *Plasmodium* 4–5
plague 6–13, 16–18, 28–29
   Antonine Plague 8–9, 28
   Black Death 12–13, 28
   Great Plague 16–17, 28
   Justinian Plague 10–12, 28
   Plague of Athens 6–7, 28
quarantine, using 17, 19–20, 23
Rome, ancient 5, 8–9, 18
sanitation 2, 7, 17, 21
smallpox 7, 9, 15, 24–25, 28–29
Snow, John 21

Spanish Flu 2–3, 22–23, 29
tuberculosis 18–19, 29
typhoid 7
typhus 7, 15
vaccines,
   BCG 19
   smallpox 25
viruses,
   coronaviruses 2–3
   Covid-19 2–3, 28–29
   ebola 29
   influenza 2–3, 7, 22–23, 29
   variola 24–25
World Health Organization 2, 24
Yellow Fever 28

Franklin Watts
First published in Great Britain in 2020 by The Watts Publishing Group

Copyright © The Watts Publishing Group, 2020

All rights reserved.

Credits
Editor: Sarah Peutrill
Designer: Jim Green
Picture researcher: Diana Morris
Consultant: Alexandra R. A. Lee, University College London

Every attempt has been made to clear copyright. Should there be any inadvertent omission please apply to the publisher for rectification.

HB ISBN: 978 1 4451 7959 9
PB ISBN: 978 1 4451 7960 5
Ebook ISBN: 9781 4451 8012 0

Printed in Dubai

Franklin Watts
An imprint of
Hachette Children's Group
Part of The Watts Publishing Group
Carmelite House
50 Victoria Embankment
London EC4Y 0DZ

An Hachette UK Company
www.hachette.co.uk
www.hachettechildrens.co.uk

MIX Paper from responsible sources
FSC® C104740

Picture credits: Alamy: Agefotostock 14t; Album 17t; Keith Corrigan 12cl; Everett Historical Collection 3t; FLHC 2 17c; GL Archive 16b; Granger Historical Picture Archive 25c; Sally & Richard Greenhill 27t; Mccool 23t; National Geographic Image Collection 11tr; Pictorial Press 21c; Jonathan O'Rouke 7c; Shawshots 22c; Adam Stoltman 27bl; Sudduetsche Zeitung 19b; 2D Alan King 17c. Getty Images: Bettmann 25t. © Look and Learn: Pat Nicolle 8t. Shutterstock: Grathas Araitas 12c; Benjaminec 11b; Blue Planet Studio 8-9bg; Nick Brundle 4b; Dneprstock 5c; Everett Collection back cover, 9cl, 15t, 22b; IR2009 19cr; Javarman 12-13bg; Jorisvo 9tr; Kateryna Kon 9bl, 9br, 18-19 bg, 18-19c, 21t; Vladimir Korostyshevskiy 8b; Kotoffel 12tb; Majivecka 11tl; Mark1987 12t; Markova 2-3 bg; Nadezda Maurmakova 2t; Netfalls Remy Muser 20-21bg; Hein Nouwens 8c, 9tl, 9cr; Channarong Pherngjanda front cover; Irina Pittore 6-7 bg; Valeriya Repina 10-11bg; RomanVX 4t; Rost9 22-23bg; Stas11 11cl; Travelerpix 3b; Weredragon 14-15 bg. Wellcome Collection, London/CC BY 4.0: 13l ; 16c, 24, 25b. Wikimedia Commons: Anon 19th c lithograph/PD 6tr; Bibliothèque Nationale, Paris/PD 13tr;Tilemahos Efthimiadis/CC2A 6bl; G. Goldsmith/PHIL PD 26t;Historia de la Republica Mexicana,Alaman, 1860/PD 15c; Le Petit Journal, 1913/PD 20b; PD published 1900 7b; PD 10c, 20t, 21b, 23c; Rocky Mountain Labs/NIAD/NIH 10b; University of Toronto/PD 16-17bg; Édouard Viênot d 1872/PD 18c;Gary van der Merwe CCA 3 27br; Tony Webster CCA 2 27bc.